SANKOFA
BLACK HERITAGE COLLECTION

BELONGING

NATALIE HODGSON

SERIES EDITOR • TOM HENDERSON

www.rubiconpublishing.com

Associate Publisher: Amy Land
Project Editor: Jessica Rose
Editorial Assistants: Kristen Lazaro, Kaitlin Tremblay
Creative Director: Jennifer Drew
Lead Designer: Sherwin Flores
Graphic Designers: Roy Casim, Robin Forsyth, Jennifer Harvey, Stacy Jarvis,
Jason Mitchell

Every reasonable effort has been made to trace the owners of copyrighted
material and to make due acknowledgement. Any errors or omissions
drawn to our attention will be gladly rectified in future editions.

15 16 17 18 19   6 5 4 3 2

ISBN: 978-1-77058-827-1

Printed in China

We Rise Together: Teachers and Teacher-Librarians supporting racialized students through culturally responsive leadership.

How can we help build more inclusive and culturally responsive schools?

How can we create a safe, inviting learning space that is culturally responsive and that will engage and motivate students?

Area I need to focus on……..	Action I will take……..

CONTENTS

BELON

Everyone wants to or needs to belong somewhere, whether it is with family, at school, or in a community. Most people want to be an important part of these groups.

Some people help to make you feel like you belong. Feeling like you belong can help to shape your identity.

What can you do to make people feel like they belong?

GING

How do the people around you shape your identity?

BLACK SETTLEMENTS IN CANADA

THINK ABOUT IT

Where do you and your family live? Find out how your family came to live in that area.

SLAVERY EXISTED IN Canada from the early 17th to the early 19th centuries. However, settlements of free Black people began to be established in the 18th century. These short reports describe some of the communities that were set up in provinces across Canada.

○ AMBER VALLEY

○ KEYSTONE

○ VICTORIA

○ ELDON DISTRICT

THE BOG
○

○○
BIRCHTOWN & PREST
TOWNSHIP

Aboriginal peoples lived on the land now known as Canada long before anybody else.

AMHERSTBURG
& ELGIN SETTLEMENT
○○ ● DRESDEN

After the War of 1812, over 500 people came to Hammonds Plains, another Black settlement in Nova Scotia. This painting from around 1835 shows a Black family in this area.

NOVA SCOTIA
BIRCHTOWN

In 1783, about 1500 people of African descent arrived in Birchtown, Nova Scotia. The town was named after General Samuel Birch. He was responsible for signing many certificates of freedom for Black people who had remained loyal to the British Crown during the American Revolutionary War. Birchtown became the largest community of free Black people outside of Africa at the time. Within the first year, the number of community members grew to over 2000. However, in 1792, many of the Black Loyalists, facing hardship, left Birchtown for Sierra Leone in West Africa, where they were offered land and self-government.

NOVA SCOTIA
PRESTON TOWNSHIP

In 1796, about 600 Jamaican Maroons were deported to Nova Scotia following their rebellion against the British colonial government. Many Maroons settled in Preston Township. They brought with them their own religion and customs. The Maroons helped build government fortifications, and they served in the local militia. Most of the Maroons later left the settlement of Preston Township for Sierra Leone.

Maroons: *descendants of people who had escaped from slavery*

PRINCE EDWARD ISLAND
THE BOG

In 1784, 16 Black servants, some of whom might have been enslaved Africans, were brought by Loyalists to Île Saint-Jean, now called Prince Edward Island. One year later, there were almost 100. The Black Islanders eventually settled throughout the island. After 1799, many moved to Charlottetown and Summerside, where they were allowed to be baptized and married legally. Many eventually gathered in an area of Charlottetown known as the "Bog," which became the primary community for Black Islanders until the 1900s.

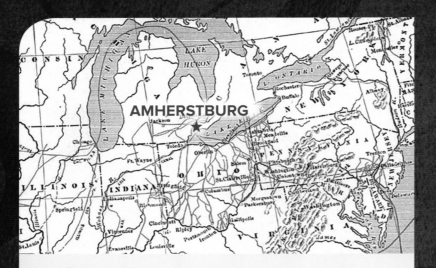

Map of part of the Underground Railroad. The Underground Railroad was not a real railroad. It was a network of secret routes and safe houses that Black people enslaved in the United States used to escape to Canada.

AMHERSTBURG

ONTARIO
AMHERSTBURG

After the War of 1812, Amherstburg was one of the most important places for enslaved Africans from the United States who were trying to get into Canada. The settlement was close to the Detroit River. Fugitives had to swim across the river in the summer or walk across it when it was frozen in the winter. Amherstburg was the busiest stop on the Underground Railroad. It was the gateway to freedom and a new life for many people. Today, Amherstburg is home to the North American Black Historical Museum.

Fugitives: *runaways*

ONTARIO
ELGIN SETTLEMENT

In 1849, William King, a Presbyterian minister, founded the Elgin Settlement in Canada. He came from the United States after his father-in-law died and left him with 15 enslaved Africans. King opposed slavery and realized he could not stay in the United States. So he took the people to Canada to build a community for them. The Elgin Settlement, also known as Buxton, became the most successful Black settlement in Canada. By the 1860s, over 2000 people lived there. The settlement became known for its independence and for its three schools and the excellent quality of education that they provided.

ONTARIO
DAWN SETTLEMENT

Josiah Henson, a former enslaved African from the United States, established the Dawn Settlement in present-day Dresden, Ontario, in 1841. In 1830, Henson escaped from slavery with his wife and four children using the Underground Railroad. He then purchased 200 acres in Dawn Township, where he established a community for former enslaved Africans. With the support of abolitionists, Henson helped establish the British American Institute, a school for people who had escaped from slavery. Because of the school, the Dawn Settlement grew to about 500 people.

abolitionists: *people who fought against slavery*

Josiah Henson

ALBERTA
AMBER VALLEY

Several hundred African Americans from Oklahoma arrived in Amber Valley in 1911 because they were denied equal rights in the United States. Most worked on farms in the area. Some people found it difficult to adjust to the harsh conditions and climate in Alberta, so they left.

SASKATCHEWAN
ELDON DISTRICT

The Eldon district was the largest Black settlement in Saskatchewan. In the early 20th century, the Canadian government offered free land in western Canada to encourage people to move west. In 1910, 12 Black families took advantage of the government's offer, and they settled in Eldon. Many were formerly enslaved Africans or descendants of formerly enslaved Africans. In 1912, settlers built the Shiloh Baptist Church as a symbol of their community. In the 1920s and 1930s, about 50 families joined the settlement. By the 1940s, many moved away looking for employment elsewhere. The Shiloh Baptist Church, however, still stands to this day.

ALBERTA
KEYSTONE

Originally known as Breton, the Keystone settlement was created in 1909 by about 1000 Black people from Oklahoma. They were looking for a place where they would have the same rights as others and be equal citizens. They began developing communities and seeking employment. However, many families were forced to leave due to natural disasters such as drought. By the 1960s, there were only six families left.

BRITISH COLUMBIA
VICTORIA

The first wave of Black settlers in British Columbia arrived in 1858. They were invited by the governor of Vancouver Island and British Columbia, James Douglas. A small group set out for Canada's west coast, where they were promised there would be no legal discrimination against them. More than 400 Black Californian families arrived by boat and built communities in Victoria and Salt Spring Island. They established small businesses and worked on farms.

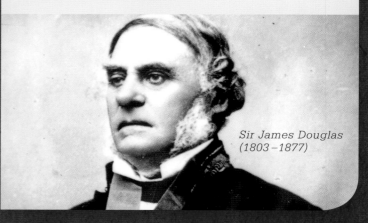

Sir James Douglas (1803–1877)

CONNECT IT

Choose one of the settlements described in these short reports and find out more information about it. In the voice of one of the settlers, write a short letter to a family member describing your new home and community.

AFRICVILLE

THINK ABOUT IT

With a partner, think about the community in which you live. How would you feel if you were forced to leave it?

AFRICVILLE WAS A small community in Nova Scotia where many people of African descent settled. Some people believe settlement in the area began over 200 years ago.

BEGINNINGS

Oral history is information about the past that is gathered from interviews with people who talk about their families and experiences. This information is often passed down orally from generation to generation.

> Historians have found records of people of African descent living in the area of Africville in 1798. But many former residents of Africville believe the community began even before then. According to the oral history of the community, there were people living in the area when Halifax was founded in 1749.

Why else might Black people have wanted to move to Canada?

> The population of Africville grew following the American Revolutionary War (1775–1783). The British colonies south of what was to become Canada were fighting for freedom from British rule. The British promised land and freedom to anyone who supported their side in the conflict. As a result, the British transported more than 3000 people of African descent to Nova Scotia and New Brunswick, and some of those Black Loyalists settled in Africville. This was land no one else had any use for yet. It was rough and rocky. Similarly, following the War of 1812 (1812–1815), Black refugees, who had been loyal to the British, were settled in Nova Scotia, and some of them found their way to Africville. The people of Africville worked as labourers, sailors, carpenters, barbers, cleaners, domestic workers, and railway porters.

View of Africville before it was destroyed in the 1960s

Africville residents did not receive the water and sewer services provided to other Halifax residents.

PLEASE
BOIL THIS
WATER BEFORE
DRINKING AND
COOKING

CHANGES

In the mid-1900s, there were about 400 people living in Africville. They had a church and their own school. Even though residents paid taxes to the city of Halifax, the city did not provide services like paved roads, running water, or street lights.

As Halifax grew, the city council began talking about needing the Africville region for industrial development. They found a use for this land that was previously thought to be useless. In 1962, the city of Halifax began formal plans for the destruction of Africville. Halifax City Council voted to move the residents to another area and bulldoze the buildings. The city council tricked people into selling their property by offering suitcases of money. These suitcases looked as if they had a lot of money, but it was not enough to make up for the loss of home and community these people faced. Attempts to save the community failed. The hard work of the community was undermined. A vibrant African Canadian community was destroyed. A piece of Canada's history was gone.

Africville residents at Seaview African United Baptist Church in 1962

REMEMBERING

Today, Africville lives on in the memories of the former residents. The Africville Genealogy Society was formed to keep those memories alive. In 1983, the society started holding annual picnics at the former site of Africville. People from all over North America began gathering to share stories and reconnect.

The former site of Africville was named a National Historic Site in 1996. It was called Seaview Park. Finally, in 2010, the city of Halifax formally apologized to the former residents and their descendants. The city promised to rebuild the church and provide money to run it as a museum. The site was renamed Africville. The museum opened in 2012. The history of Africville lives on.

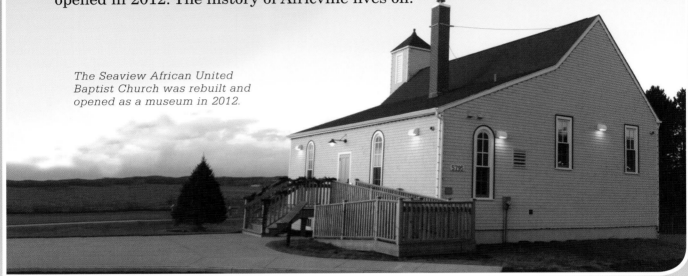

The Seaview African United Baptist Church was rebuilt and opened as a museum in 2012.

The Seaview African United Baptist Church before it was destroyed

THE OFFICIAL APOLOGY

When he was mayor of Halifax, Peter Kelly apologized to former residents of Africville for the destruction of their community.

As you read this apology, think about what the city of Halifax apologized for and what it did not apologize for.

On behalf of the Halifax Regional Municipality, I apologize to the former Africville residents and their descendants for what they have endured for almost 50 years, ever since the loss of their community …

You lost your houses, your church, all of the places where you gathered with family and friends to mark the milestones of your lives.

For all that, we apologize.

We apologize to the community elders, including those who did not live to see this day, for the pain and loss of dignity you experienced.

We apologize to the generations who followed, for the deep wounds you have inherited and the way your lives were disrupted by the disappearance of your community.

We apologize for the heartache experienced at the loss of the Seaview United Baptist Church, the spiritual heart of the community, removed in the middle of the night. We acknowledge the tremendous importance the church had, both for the congregation and the community as a whole.

We realize words cannot undo what has been done, but we are profoundly sorry and apologize to all the former residents and their descendants.

The repercussions of what happened in Africville linger to this day. They haunt us in the form of lost opportunities for young people who were never nurtured in the rich traditions, culture, and heritage of Africville.

How would you feel if your community was from Africville and you read this apology letter?

They play out in lingering feelings of hurt and distrust, emotions that this municipality continues to work hard with the African Nova Scotian community to overcome.

For all the distressing consequences, we apologize.

Our history cannot be rewritten but, thankfully, the future is a blank page and, starting today, we hold the pen with which we can write a shared tomorrow.

It is in that spirit of respect and reconciliation that we ask your forgiveness.

CONNECT IT

Find out more about Africville. Using your research, write a letter in the voice of a resident to the Halifax City Council before the community was destroyed explaining why it would be a mistake to destroy Africville.

HIDDEN
TREASURE

BY NATASHA HENRY

THINK ABOUT IT

What do you know about your family's history? Did your ancestors move to Canada from another country? Ask older family members for some information about your family's history.

WHEN JAMAL, ANNIE, AND MICHELLE decide to play hide-and-seek, they're just looking to have a little fun. But when they hide in the attic, they stumble upon an old shoebox ...

Read this reader's theatre script see what they really find.

CHARACTERS:

Narrator

Annie

Jamal

Michelle

Mom

Narrator:	It's a dark and stormy Saturday at the Warner house. It's the perfect day for a game of hide-and-seek.
Sound Effect (SFX):	Thunder booms overhead.
Annie *(counting while her brother and sister hide)*:	One … two … three … four …
Michelle *(looking upward)*:	Let's hide in the attic!
Jamal:	The attic? THE ATTIC? No way! Absolutely not! There's no chance —
Michelle:	Oh, come on! What's the worst thing that could be up there?
Jamal:	I bet there are cobwebs and HUGE spiders with big, ugly eyes. And bats! If I were a bat, I'd live in an attic. There's lots of spiders to eat.
Annie *(continuing to count)*:	Twenty … twenty-one … twenty-two … twenty-three …
Michelle:	Hurry! We're running out of time.
Narrator:	Jamal and Michelle climb the stairs to the attic.
SFX:	CLOMP! CLOMP! CLOMP!
Michelle:	See! It's not so bad up here.
Jamal:	See? I can't see a thing in here!
Michelle:	There must be a light somewhere. Aha! Found it …
Narrator:	The light comes on a second too late. Jamal trips over an old shoebox.
Jamal:	WHOOOAAAAA!
SFX:	THUD!
Michelle:	You're so clumsy! Look at all this stuff. Who knew Mom and Dad were hiding so much junk up here?

Jamal: And look at all these old photos. That woman looks a lot like Mom.

Narrator: Annie and Mom rush upstairs to see what's going on. They find Jamal and Michelle examining the contents of the shoebox.

Mom: What's all the commotion up here? Is everyone okay?

Jamal: I'm fine. Hey, Mom. Who are all the people in these photos?

Mom: Wow! I haven't seen those photos in years. They are old photographs from my grandmother's house. The people are all members of our family. They came from the United States in the early 1900s to a community called Eldon.

Annie: Where's the Eldon district?

Mom: It's near Maidstone, Saskatchewan. That's just about an hour from here.

Michelle: I think I've heard of it. We've been learning about Black communities across Canada in Ms. Mohammed's class. I didn't know our family was from one of them.

Mom: It is. Saskatchewan and Alberta had just joined Canada. Those provinces, along with Manitoba, invited people from the United States, Europe, and other parts of Canada to settle in the new provinces.

Annie: Who's this?

Mom: That's a photo of your great-grandfather in the 1930s. His parents were two of the 1300 Black men, women, and children who immigrated to Canada's western provinces.

Jamal: Why did people want to come to Canada?

Mom: Black people in the United States were experiencing a lot of racism. Some laws and customs, referred to as Jim Crow, were passed. These laws and customs restricted the rights of African Americans. Under Jim Crow, Black and White people could not even shake hands. Your great-great-grandparents also believed that moving to Canada would be safer and would provide a better future for their families.

Michelle: People couldn't even shake hands? That's awful!

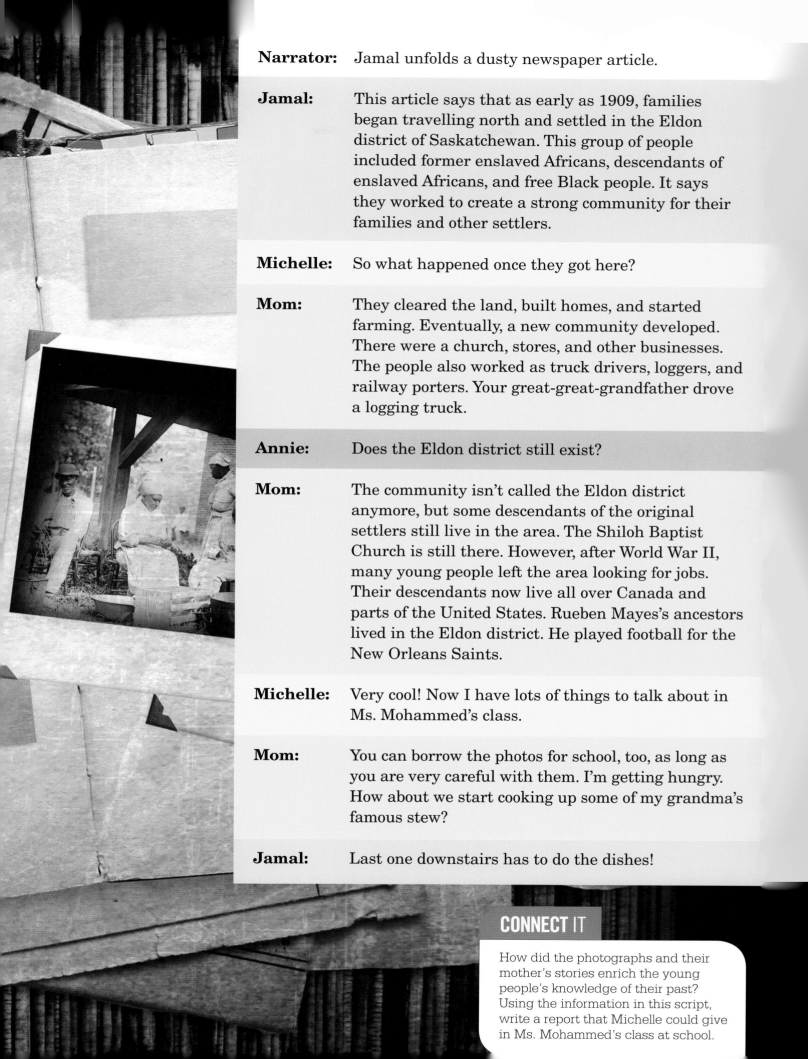

Narrator: Jamal unfolds a dusty newspaper article.

Jamal: This article says that as early as 1909, families began travelling north and settled in the Eldon district of Saskatchewan. This group of people included former enslaved Africans, descendants of enslaved Africans, and free Black people. It says they worked to create a strong community for their families and other settlers.

Michelle: So what happened once they got here?

Mom: They cleared the land, built homes, and started farming. Eventually, a new community developed. There were a church, stores, and other businesses. The people also worked as truck drivers, loggers, and railway porters. Your great-great-grandfather drove a logging truck.

Annie: Does the Eldon district still exist?

Mom: The community isn't called the Eldon district anymore, but some descendants of the original settlers still live in the area. The Shiloh Baptist Church is still there. However, after World War II, many young people left the area looking for jobs. Their descendants now live all over Canada and parts of the United States. Rueben Mayes's ancestors lived in the Eldon district. He played football for the New Orleans Saints.

Michelle: Very cool! Now I have lots of things to talk about in Ms. Mohammed's class.

Mom: You can borrow the photos for school, too, as long as you are very careful with them. I'm getting hungry. How about we start cooking up some of my grandma's famous stew?

Jamal: Last one downstairs has to do the dishes!

CONNECT IT

How did the photographs and their mother's stories enrich the young people's knowledge of their past? Using the information in this script, write a report that Michelle could give in Ms. Mohammed's class at school.

Jackson Holland (right) chats with relatives.

GREAT-GREAT-GREAT-GRANDSON
REMEMBERS

JACKSON HOLLAND
CBC HAMILTON
16 JULY 2012

THINK ABOUT IT

Why is it important for a person to know about his or her family's history?

FIFTEEN-YEAR-OLD Jackson Holland lives in Hamilton, Ontario. He has family living all over North America. Holland's great-great-great-grandfather was Thomas John Holland. He escaped from slavery in the United States and came to Canada in 1860, when he was only 15 years old.

Recently, hundreds of Holland's relatives gathered for a family reunion. They met in Hamilton, the city where Thomas John Holland first lived as a free person. Read this article written by Holland to learn more about his family and their reunion.

This weekend, my extended family, some 250 strong, left footprints across Canada, the United States, and Bermuda as they made the journey to Hamilton, Ontario, to honour Thomas John's courage, his selflessness, and his memory. And to learn more about the place he called home.

It was a three-day reunion that began with a boat cruise in my city's harbour, followed by dancing and a massive gathering in Dundurn Park. Saturday was a perfect sun-filled day for a picnic. Scattered among the aunts, uncles, and cousins was a smattering of media. People gathered around to listen as others were interviewed, hearing inspiring and thought-provoking stories.

I saw the darling little face of the youngest member of the family, who is only four months old, and the time-worn face of a 95-year-old man, the oldest relative at the picnic.

smattering: *small number of*

> Why might Holland and members of his family want to know about the place their ancestors called home?

George Campbell, of Maryland, was the oldest person to attend the family reunion in Hamilton. He is pictured here with one of the youngest attendees, Michaela, from North Carolina.

Greetings from President Obama

It was so exciting to read President Barack Obama's message to us, greeting our entire family and wishing us a wonderful reunion.

There were so many people, so accomplished in almost every conceivable area: arts, music, business, education, and intercultural relations. The list goes on and on. So many relatives are working to make a better world.

Little ones ran around giggling, kids squirted each other with water guns while others — some who had only just met each other for the first time — played football and soccer together.

Everyone was snapping photos with everything from expensive long lenses to video cameras and cellphones, all to capture precious moments and the faces of a sea of relatives.

Scores of cousins walked across York Street to the Hamilton Cemetery and stood reflecting over Thomas John Holland and his wife Henrietta's gravesite.

conceivable: *imaginable*

> **To be among so many high achievers motivates me. Knowing I'm the next chapter of this story of history, courage, and success in my family reassures me that I'm here to do great things, because it's in me — strength is in my soul and it's in my blood.**

Members go through family photos.

Holland-Howard family members pose for a photograph.

The high point of the day for me: watching a photographer climb atop an SUV to take a family photo that captured the hundreds of smiling faces.

I was inspired by the stories of achievement and awed by the numbers of people whom I can call my family. It was astonishing to learn so much about my ancestors and what they have accomplished.

To be among so many high achievers motivates me. Knowing I'm the next chapter of this story of history, courage, and success in my family reassures me that I'm here to do great things, because it's in me — strength is in my soul and it's in my blood.

◄ What do you think Holland means when he says strength is in his blood?

CONNECT IT

Why was this family reunion so important to Jackson Holland? Send him a short email explaining why you found his article inspiring.

BEGINN

BY NIKKI GRIMES

IN THIS POEM, Nikki Grimes writes about a friendship that develops between a young girl and a boy who moves to her neighbourhood.

I.
Jake moved to the
neighbourhood
Right after his dad moved out
And left his mom a mess.
One December day, at recess
I found him all by himself,
Clinging to a swing,
Crying in the cold.
I plopped down on the swing
Next to him,
Pushed myself off the ground,
And kept him quiet company.
When I could see
He was done crying,
I said, "Hi. My name's Joy."
And he said, between sniffles,
"I'm Jake."
And that's all it took
To make us friends forever.

NGS

II.
When I had appendicitis
And thought I might die,
I woke up after surgery
And there was Jake
Staring down at me,
Saying "Hey!"
Which was about
All the conversation
I was in the mood for.

III.
These days,
We're mostly basketball buddies.
Jake doesn't talk much,
But the silences between us
Are filled with friendship.
I don't know what I'd do
Without him.

CONNECT IT

With a partner, talk about why Joy and Jake had such a strong friendship. What did each one give to and get from the other? With a partner, write a short rap that describes what friendship means to you.

HARRIET'S DAUGHTER

BY MARLENE NOURBESE PHILIP

THINK ABOUT IT

Have you, or anyone you know, ever moved to a new school? In a small group, discuss how difficult it can be to adjust to a new environment.

THE NOVEL *HARRIET'S DAUGHTER* tells the story of Zulma, a young girl who moves to Canada from Tobago, and how a new friend, Margaret, supports her as she gets to know her new home. In this excerpt from the novel, Margaret describes how she helps Zulma feel like she belongs in her new community.

ABOUT THE AUTHOR

Marlene NourbeSe Philip was born in Tobago in 1947. She is a writer who now lives in Toronto. Her stories and poems have won many awards, and are featured in magazines and journals around the world. *Harriet's Daughter* is her first novel.

Zulma really didn't know much about anything — about living and going to school in Toronto, I mean. Like she didn't even know what a transfer was and was paying twice, sometimes three times to get round on the buses and subways. I set her straight on that one and even showed her how she could make stopovers on the same transfer, if she was continuing on in the same direction. She knew a lot, and I mean a lot, about Tobago and things like the mango season; why it was better to plant some crops at full moon and not at new moon; and how to kill a chicken, clean it, and season it. None of this was any good to her in Toronto, or at school, so I began looking out for her, making sure other kids didn't push her around.

Most of the time, she was unhappy, really unhappy. Her problems made mine look like nothing. When her mother left the island, Zulma was three, and she went to live with her gran. Her mother went back for a visit five years ago and that was the last time Zulma had seen her. In that time, her mother had got a new husband, her stepfather, and Zulma did not get along with him. He didn't like her either. There were lots of fights; she missed her gran, and didn't want to be in Canada, especially in the winter! I didn't get along with my parents either, but at least I didn't know anything better or anywhere else, except the bloody icy playground and the streets around my home. But Zulma? She talked of beaches and blue sea, sunshine and coconut trees, and days being so hot the asphalt would melt, and a gran who thought she was the most important person in the world. If I were in her shoes, I would have gone mad, or maybe run away, but she didn't. At least she had me.

It was maybe a month after she and I had become friends that the Veep — the Vice-Principal — sent for me. I hadn't been caught throwing snowballs recently, so I was pretty sure he wasn't going to bawl me out or put me in the hall, but I was still a little worried. …

> What picture does the narrator create of Zulma in this paragraph?

bloody: *word used in informal language to emphasize an idea or show annoyance*

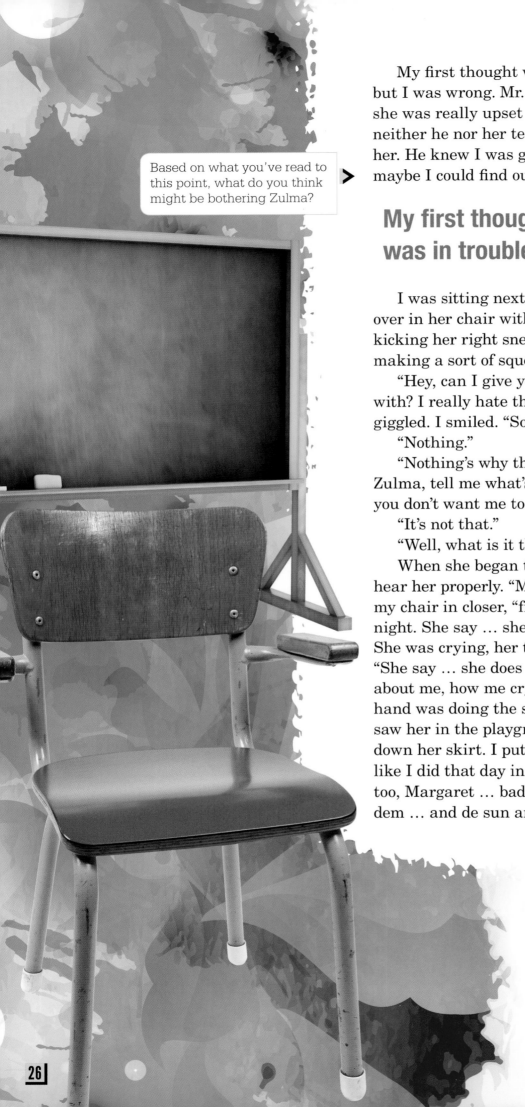

Based on what you've read to this point, what do you think might be bothering Zulma?

My first thought was that Zulma was in trouble, but I was wrong. Mr. Dunkirk explained to me that she was really upset about something but that neither he nor her teacher could get anything from her. He knew I was good friends with her, he said, so maybe I could find out so that they could help her. ...

My first thought was that Zulma was in trouble, but I was wrong.

I was sitting next to Zulma. She was hunched over in her chair with her head down, and she was kicking her right sneaker against the tiled floor, making a sort of squeaky noise.

"Hey, can I give you my North Stars to do that with? I really hate them." She looked over at me and giggled. I smiled. "So, what's up?"

"Nothing."

"Nothing's why the Veep sent for me, right? C'mon Zulma, tell me what's up? You know I won't talk if you don't want me to."

"It's not that."

"Well, what is it then?"

When she began to talk, it was so low I couldn't hear her properly. "Me a get ... one letter ...," I pulled my chair in closer, "from me ggg ... gran ... last night. She say ... she say ... she mmiss me ..." She was crying, her tears dropping on to her skirt. "She say ... she does ... dream ... every night ... about me, how me crying and not happy." Her right hand was doing the same thing it did the day I first saw her in the playground, she was wiping it up and down her skirt. I put my arm around her shoulders, like I did that day in the playground. "Me miss she too, Margaret ... bad bad ... de goats and de chickens dem ... and de sun and ..."

"Zulma" — I don't know why but I was whispering — "Zulma," I said again, "I promise you, by the end of the year you will be back in Tobago. I promise I'll get you there." Why I said what I said I still don't know, except that I just wanted to help her, and didn't like to see her sad. I believed my promise, though. We both believed my promise. I had no money; I didn't know how I was going to help her to get back to Tobago without money, but I was the only person who wanted to help her. We didn't talk about it any more, but it was there between us. …

I'm pretty sure it was on the way home that day (I had asked Zulma to spend the night at my place) that I began to learn Tobago-talk from Zulma. When I first met Zulma, I didn't understand much of what she said, especially when she talked quickly, which was often. Within two or three weeks though, I was understanding most of what she was saying. Her talk had all these hills and valleys, nothing like my flat, old, boring Canadian talk. Where I would say I, she would say me, or ah; where I said her, she would say she; but that was only the beginning of how we talked differently, although it was supposed to be English we both spoke.

When I asked her on the way home that evening to teach me Tobago-talk (that was what I called it), she got all quiet and serious; she didn't say anything for a while. Then "Is what you want to talk like that for? You speak nice already."

"I like the way you talk. I want to talk like that. Sometimes I hear my mother on the phone with her Jamaican friends; when they get going, I can hardly understand them."

"Your mother talk dialect?"

A dialect is a form of a language spoken in a particular area. Why are dialects important for a sense of belonging?

"Yep, but she likes to pretend she doesn't know how to; she thinks it's better to sound like a Canadian. In any case, after a while you begin to lose your accent you know, like you're doing." I nudged her and smiled.

"Me? Never! Me never going lose me accent. I'se a Tobagonian and I'se proud of it."

"All right, all right, I'm sorry." I laughed. "I didn't mean to insult you." It was real important to Zulma to believe in where she came from and who she was — Tobagonian. I had forgotten that. To say she was sounding less Tobagonian might mean she was growing away from her gran and Tobago. Her gran might not understand her. Yet I knew she liked her classes where she learned English, what I called flat English or plain English, no hills or valleys.

"Well, I want to talk like you … if you'll teach me."

"You serious?"

"Uh-huh, then I'll be bilingual."

"Oh all right. When you want start?"

"Now. How would you say, 'I want to go to the movies'?"

"Me a want go to de movies."

"Me a want go to the movies."

"No, not the but de, de movies."

That was how our lessons in Tobago-talk started. She never said anything, but I knew that Zulma was very proud to be teaching me her talk. I was always telling her stuff, and explaining to her how things went, like why it was important for her not to ever wear those blue satin ribbons again; but now she could teach me something. When we did our lessons in Tobago-talk, she looked really happy.

CONNECT IT

Imagine you are a new student at your school. Write a journal entry about the experience. Consider what it might take to fit in or to make friends.

NOT ALLOWED!

JOHN GODDARD
THE TORONTO STAR
16 FEBRUARY 2009

ONE DAY IN 1945, two friends decided to go skating. Little did they know that they would not be allowed into the rink because of racism. But they would not let racism get them down.

THINK ABOUT IT

What would you do if you were told you could take part in an activity but your friend couldn't? Would you participate or leave? Explain your answer to a partner.

Harry Gairey and Donny Jubas decided to go skating. They were 15 years old.

"Harry was going to teach me how to skate," Jubas recalls of a gorgeous winter day on Saturday, 22 November 1945, a watershed date in Toronto race relations.

"I wasn't a great skater," Gairey says, "but I was good enough to show my buddy and have fun."

Instead of going to the outdoor rink in their College-Spadina area, they set out for the more glamorous Icelandia indoor arena on Yonge St., north of St. Clair Ave.

Neither had been there before.

"I go up to buy tickets and the guy says to me, 'We can't sell your friend a ticket,'" Jubas recalls, incomprehension surging in his voice.

"I turn around and look behind me, then I turn back and say, 'Are you talking to me?'

"And he says, 'Yeah, I'm talking to you. We don't sell tickets to Negroes. We don't let them in here. So do you want only one ticket?'"

"And I turn and say, 'Let's get out of here.'"

incomprehension: *lack of understanding*

Gairey, who is Black, and Jubas, who is Jewish, are pushing 80 now.

They were kids taken by surprise in 1945, but they've long since known that adult Blacks in Toronto in 1945 — Jews as well — were attuned to the city's unspoken race restrictions.

Certain beaches were understood to be off limits. Certain restaurants were known to keep some diners waiting indefinitely. The Icelandia, they later discovered, often turned away Jews as well.

But until the moment at the ticket booth, the boys had been spared such realities.

"Like a slap in the face," Jubas says.

"I always remember it," says Gairey.

When Gairey returned home that day, he told his mother, who told his father, Harry Gairey Sr., a railroad porter with a reputation for standing up for his rights. "I was crazy for a moment," Gairey Sr. later recalled in a memoir, *A Black Man's Toronto*.

> A memoir is a personal account written about one's past experiences.

That Monday morning, he went to see his alderman, who got him an appointment the next day to address city council and Mayor Robert Saunders, a populist known as "Grassroots Bob." Let Black boys be banned from the Icelandia, Gairey Sr. told them, if they will be exempt from fighting in the next war.

"But, Your Worship and gentlemen of the council, it's not going to be that way," the father said. "You're going to say he's a Canadian and you'll conscript him. And if so, I would like my son to have everything that a Canadian citizen is entitled to."

On Thursday, the *Toronto Daily Star* ran a sympathetic interview with the boy.

> What do you think a sympathetic interview is? Why would one be important?

On Friday, the paper carried a story saying 25 University of Toronto students picketed the Icelandia carrying signs saying, "Colour Prejudice Must Go" and "Racial discrimination should not be tolerated."

It took another two years, but as a result of the Icelandia refusing a ticket to Harry Gairey Jr., Toronto City Council passed an ordinance against discrimination based on race, creed, colour, or religion.

The Icelandia has long since closed.

Gairey Sr. went on to become one of the most prominent activists of his generation, a lifelong promoter of Black rights. He died at 98 in 1993.

Three years later in his honour, the neighbourhood rink where his son and Jubas normally skated as children, at Bathurst St. just south of Dundas St. W., was renamed the Harry Ralph Gairey Ice Rink.

At the naming ceremony, Gairey Jr. and Jubas rekindled their childhood friendship and have been meeting monthly for lunch ever since.

---

attuned: *aware of*
alderman: *member of a town or city government*
ordinance: *law*

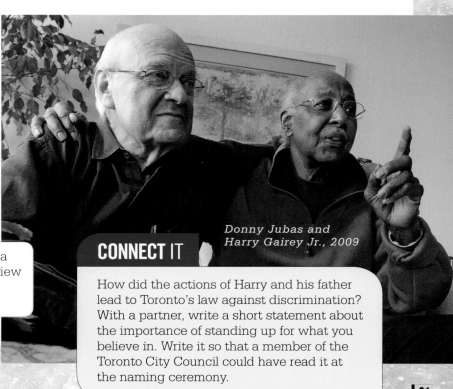

Donny Jubas and Harry Gairey Jr., 2009

CONNECT IT

How did the actions of Harry and his father lead to Toronto's law against discrimination? With a partner, write a short statement about the importance of standing up for what you believe in. Write it so that a member of the Toronto City Council could have read it at the naming ceremony.

Celebrating HISTORY

THINK ABOUT IT

In a small group, share why you think it is important to have organizations that celebrate African Canadian history.

BRITISH COLUMBIA BLACK HISTORY AWARENESS SOCIETY

Founding Year: 1994

Where: Victoria, British Columbia

Initiative: This organization celebrates the achievements of Black pioneers in BC. It works to increase awareness of the history of Black people.

Goals: This organization aims to develop an interest in promoting and educating people about Black history in BC. The society also promotes diversity and inclusion in the province. It works to encourage young people and children to develop their interest in the achievements of Black people in both BC and the rest of the country.

Fast Fact: In 1998, the BC Black History Awareness Society developed a school curriculum about the history of Black pioneers. It also established a Learning Centre website where anyone can learn about interesting facts, places, and events in BC's Black history.

BLACK SETTLERS OF ALBERTA AND SASKATCHEWAN HISTORICAL SOCIETY

Founding Year: 2005

Where: Edmonton, Alberta

Initiative: This organization works to pay tribute to Black settlers. It archives and preserves their stories of struggle and success in the history of Canada.

Goals: This organization aims to educate, promote, and recognize the historic role Black settlers played in developing the lands that would become Alberta and Saskatchewan.

Fast Fact: This organization was founded by four women. They are all descendants of Black enslaved Africans and early Canadian settlers.

The Ware homestead near Brooks, Alberta, home of John Ware, one of the first cowboys in Alberta

SASKATCHEWAN AFRICAN CANADIAN HERITAGE MUSEUM

Founding Year: 2002

Where: Regina, Saskatchewan

Initiative: This charitable organization and virtual museum works to strengthen and preserve Black history in Saskatchewan through the inclusion and the celebration of diversity.

Goals: This organization aims to research and highlight the achievements and contributions of Black people in the province's history and to educate people about and celebrate their history.

Fast Fact: The museum started as an informal organization. By 2004, it was officially recognized as a non-profit corporation.

CANADIAN MULTICULTURAL DISABILITY CENTRE

Founding Year: 1996

Where: Winnipeg, Manitoba

Initiative: This community-based organization works to improve the quality of lives of Canadians with disabilities. It has a focus on people from diverse backgrounds.

Goals: This organization aims to help persons with disabilities fully participate in Canadian life by providing opportunities and developing their skills and education. The organization works to educate others about the role of cultural diversity in developing opportunities for persons with disabilities.

Fast Fact: The centre is partnered with over 20 organizations across Canada in support of people of different ethnicities living with a disability.

ONTARIO BLACK HISTORY SOCIETY

Founding Year: 1978

Where: Toronto, Ontario

Initiative: This non-profit charity is the only Ontario Provincial Heritage Organization devoted to Black history and heritage.

Goals: This organization aims to increase interest in Black history. It recognizes, preserves, and promotes the contributions of Black people and promoting Black history in school curriculums.

Fast Fact: This award-winning organization received the African Canadian Achievement Award.

BLACK LOYALIST HERITAGE SOCIETY

Founding Year: 1989

Where: Birchtown, Nova Scotia

Initiative: It is the only national charitable organization that preserves the contributions of Black Loyalists within Canada's cultural heritage.

Goals: This organization aims to develop, preserve, promote, and protect the history and heritage of the Black Loyalists and their descendants. The society celebrates the survival and determination of the Black Loyalists in Canada. The organization also participates in multicultural campaigns and projects.

Fast Fact: In 2000, the society opened the Black Loyalist Museum. It is located in the Birchtown Old School House. The Black Loyalist Heritage Society was recognized as an official charity in 2001.

CONNECT IT

With a partner, research another organization devoted to celebrating Black history or the history of another cultural group in Canada. Prepare a fact card similar to the fact cards in this selection. Share your fact card with another pair of students.

Names

In a small group, discuss where your name came from if you know. If you don't know, ask an adult who might know the story behind your name.

NAMES GIVE US a sense of belonging. Names can connect us to our culture and our ancestors. Your name is a part of your identity. Some families celebrate with special rituals often known as naming ceremonies when selecting a name for a newborn.

Where do our names come from? In many cultures, children are given the names of their parents, grandparents, or other ancestors. Choosing a name for a child has a significant meaning and purpose for many families. Did you know that names can tell a story about a person? Children are named for a variety of reasons, such as the day of the week they were born, if their parents had been wanting a baby for a long time, to express the character of the child, and so on.

In some African societies, people have naming ceremonies to welcome new babies into families and communities. This naming process is very important, and elders play a significant role in this custom. Elders are extremely respected in African culture, and are invited to speak first at all ceremonies, including naming ceremonies.

Naming ceremonies are joyous events with lots of music and positive energy. They always take place in a clean house or space and begin with a libation. A libation is a ritual that involves pouring water into a plant, a flower vase, or on the floor to give thanks to supreme beings, gods, or ancestors. A libation is also a way to connect with ancestors. Naming ceremonies usually end with drumming, dancing, eating good food, and thanking everyone for attending.

Lost Names

Africans who were brought to North America as enslaved people were stripped of their African names. Slave owners gave these people new names that were common in European cultures, and they often gave their own names. Today, some Black people in North America are giving their children African names to help them connect with their roots.

I'm Still Abeo

My name is Abeo, which means "her birth brings happiness." I was only 12 years old when I was taken from my family.

It was a scorching hot sunny day. Mama sent me to fetch some water, and off I went with my basket in hand. Mama always sends me out with lots of time because she knows I like to go wandering. I followed a familiar path and stopped under a mahogany tree, where I sat for a while. *(Laughing)* I love playing with dirt between my toes.

I decided to head back home when I heard footsteps and voices drawing near. I tiptoed backwards into a bush, but I was grabbed, chained, and put on the end of a long line of sad faces. I tried to look ahead for familiar faces and saw my uncle way up front, but I didn't see anyone else I knew.

We were forced onto a huge ship like animals. I was begging one of the White men to let me go back to my family. I was so scared! But his [tongue doesn't] speak what my tongue speaks.

We spent weeks at sea. Hungry … Sick … Crowded … Angry … Afraid … Then we were taken off the boat and sold to the highest bidder. They examined my legs, my back, my hands, and my teeth. But I don't know why.

I was given a new name. They call me Emma, but I'm still Abeo!

I worked long hours in the White man's house, scrubbing floors, cooking, cleaning, and doing laundry.

Oh how I miss my mama and how she used to braid my hair, softly singing, "Abeo, Abeo brings me joy … *(Crying)* Abeo, Abeo brings me joy."

In written versions of plays and monologues, characters' actions are often set in italics. This is so that the actors and readers know which text should be read and which text should be performed.

What do you think Abeo means when she says that his tongue doesn't "speak what my tongue speaks"?

CONNECT IT

Go online and research names other than your own that you think express your personality. Write about why these names capture parts of your personality.

WHY ANANSI HAS EIGHT THIN LEGS

A TRADITIONAL STORY

LEARNING ABOUT THEIR ancestors' customs and traditions helps people to feel like they belong to their culture, family, and community. Staying connected to our cultural past gives us something to be proud of and knowledge to share with others. Sharing folk tales is an oral tradition that unites people of all ages.

Stories are passed from one generation to the next. They help us learn morals. African folklore includes the stories, tales, and legends that are an important part of African culture. Many cultures have folk tales in their histories.

Read the following African folk tale about a trickster spider named Anansi (also spelled Ananse, Kwaku Ananse, and Anancy). Anansi stories originated with the Akan People of West Africa. These tales are very popular in West Africa and the West Indies.

This is the story of Anansi the spider. Anansi has been given a special power by the Sky God — the power of storytelling so that he can spin stories about life on Earth. The tale you will read today is about how Anansi has eight thin legs. You see, he used to be very big, and had huge, thick legs. Why, he could scare any creature in the forest.

It all started one day when Anansi went to see Rabbit. Anansi smelled something yummy coming from Rabbit's house. "Are those greens cooking in your pot? Yum!" said Anansi.

"Yes they are," Rabbit replied. "It's a family tradition, you know. We prepare our greens ever so slowly to preserve all the flavour. They should be finished shortly. Stick around and we can have a nice meal together."

But Anansi didn't want to wait. So he instead suggested another idea. "I know. I'll tie a web going from your pot to my leg. That way, when the meal's ready, you can pull on it and let me know."

Rabbit agreed and off Anansi went spinning his web.

Just as he finished tying his web to Rabbit's pot, Anansi smelled another delightful aroma. "I know that smell," he thought. "It's homemade beans!"

The smell was coming from Wild Boar's house. Anansi scurried over to the tree house, where Wild Boar greeted him. "Please stay and have something to eat with us. It shouldn't take much longer."

In case you haven't noticed, Anansi was a little impatient — he hated waiting to eat. So Anansi made the same suggestion to Wild Boar that he had for Rabbit.

Wild Boar agreed with Anansi's plan. So Anansi started spinning more of his web.

All of a sudden, Anansi noticed another smell. Past the river, he saw Monkey outside his house with a huge pot on an open fire. Anansi inched his way across the river. "Hello, Monkey! Smells like you're making sweet potatoes with honey."

"You have a nose like a lion," Monkey chuckled. "Now have a seat and be patient. My sweet potatoes with honey are almost ready."

What do you think Anansi suggested to Monkey? That's exactly right. He proposed that he would tie a string of his web around one of his legs and the other end to Monkey's pot. Monkey agreed to this, but advised Anansi that he might want to tie the web to a few of his legs to be sure he'd feel the tugging.

So Anansi hurried along up his web to a spot that was an equal distance from all of the pots.

What do you predict is going to happen to Anansi? >

He ended up over
the river. Then, taking
Monkey's advice, he made sure all
of his legs were tied to a piece of the web.
Two of his legs were tied to the string of web
on Rabbit's greens, three of his legs were tied to
the string for Wild Boar's beans, and his last three
legs were tied to Monkey's pot. There he was in the
middle of his web, with his legs tied in different directions.
Anansi thought his plan was clever.

Just then, the web on two of his legs started tugging.
"Oh, oh, this is great! Rabbit's greens are ready!" He
started to crawl in the direction of Rabbit's house, but
suddenly there was a tug on three of his legs. "The sweet
potatoes are ready too!" Finally, the last three strings
attached to his last three legs were pulled.

Anansi screamed, "Oh, oh, ouch! My legs! They're being
stretched! They're becoming so skinny! I can't hold onto
my web anymore!" Anansi fell into the river. The river
cleaned the webs off him. Luckily, Anansi was able crawl
out of the water. "This was
a terrible idea!" he cried. ◄ What is the moral of
this story?

That is how Anansi
came to have eight thin legs.

CONNECT IT

With a partner, create a new
story about Anansi. Remember
that traditional stories should
have a moral and that they
are meant to be passed along
orally. Practise reading your
story aloud to your class.

TORONTO'S 1ST AFRICENTRIC SCHOOL

1430
SHEPPARD PUBLIC SCHOOL

IN 2009, the first public Africentric school opened its doors in Ontario. Africentric schools focus on teaching African Canadian students about their heritage. This is so that students can be proud of that heritage. They also work to get students excited about learning. Read this article and interview. You'll find out all about Africentric schools. You'll also read about how they are working toward strengthening the African Canadian community.

On Tuesday, when hundreds of thousands of Ontario students head back to school, a lot of attention will be focused on one particular school in Toronto's north end.

It only has 85 students, but hopes are high for the Africentric Alternative School…

The administrative staff, the teachers, the parents — even the kids — are excited about the new school.

"I'm going to learn how to write the A, B, C, Ds," says Makeba Ofori-McRae in anticipation.

When Makeba enters grade one she wants to "learn how to write the numbers. Then I'm going to colour."

Her mother, Amma, says she enrolled Makeba in the Africentric school so her daughter would be taught about her Black heritage.

"It's just something that they're going to be learning," she said. "It's got nothing to do with separating. We're still going to be around other people."

Thando Hyman-Aman, the principal of the Africentric school, is adamant the children will learn the same curriculum as all other schools in Ontario.

anticipation: *excitement about something that is going to take place*

"The same reading, the same writing, the same mathematics will be there," she said.

"What makes this school look different are the culturally relevant resources that we use." …

"We definitely want to nurture a sense of belonging and community, but we also want to make sure that our standards are very high — where students can read, write, speak clearly, and perform very well," said Hyman-Aman.

Leah Newbold, the school's French, health and phys-ed teacher, is also excited about the new school.

"I know that the students in our communities are brilliant, and I want to be part of a school that's helping them to demonstrate that — and that's leading them to be successful."

> How do you think Africentric schools would help students feel like they belong?

AN INTERVIEW WITH
GEORGE DEI

GEORGE DEI IS a professor at the University of Toronto. He focuses on issues such as race and racism. In 2009, he sat down with Scott Anderson of the *University of Toronto Magazine* to talk about Africentric schools and why they are important in today's society.

What is an Africentric school?

The current school system looks at the world through European eyes. We're talking about looking at the world through the eyes of African peoples — their experiences, their cultural knowledge, and their history.

Africentric education sees schooling as a community endeavour, which means that parents, students, administrators, educators, and governments share in the responsibility to ensure success. In the existing system, students are treated as individual learners. We want them to see themselves as a community of learners with a responsibility to those who are struggling. We want the "A" students to assist those who are not doing as well.

How will the school's curriculum differ?

Of course, students need to know about European history. But they also must understand that African history is central to the construction of European history. You cannot present world history in a way that leaves out a group of people or says that their history doesn't matter.

What has research indicated about the performance of Black students who attend an Africentric school versus those who attend a regular public school?

Black students at Africentric schools perform better on tests, skip class less often, show greater respect for authority and elders, report feeling a greater sense of belonging in their schools, and have a greater commitment to social responsibility and community welfare.

endeavour: *effort aimed at achieving a goal*

If Africentric schools are seen as a solution, what are they a solution to?

High dropout rates, low motivation, teachers' low expectations of some students, stereotyping of Black, religious minority, and working-class students, a lack of respect for authority, and a lack of student commitment to community.

Would resources be better directed at solving the problems in all schools rather than creating a separate school?

It cannot be an "either/or" solution. It has to be "and/with." In 1979, I attended a meeting of the Organization of Parents of Black Children in Toronto. The parents were speaking about the school system failing their children. In 2009, parents [were] still talking about this. It was time to try a new approach.

CONNECT IT

With a partner, make a list of the benefits for students attending Africentric schools and a list of the benefits for these same students attending non-Africentric schools.

CELEBRATING
Caribbean
CULTURE

THINK ABOUT IT

What celebrations are you aware of in your community? Where do these celebrations take place? With a partner, discuss how each celebration helps form a feeling of belonging within the community.

PARADES AND FESTIVALS are a great way to celebrate your culture with your community. Many communities across Canada celebrate together by hosting festivals where they can showcase their unique food, music, dance, dress, and ways of having fun. Read the following report to learn about carnivals that celebrate culture in Canada.

CARIFIESTA
Montreal

Established in 1974, Carifiesta is a carnival in Montreal for people to experience the joy and happiness of Caribbean culture. The parade features floats, traditional dances, and elaborate costumes. The floats are decorated to reflect the many different countries represented in Carifiesta. Music is an integral part to the carnival, so many bands perform. The Junior Carnival is held a week before the main parade. It shows younger children some of the things found in Caribbean culture. Carifiesta celebrates and educates people about Caribbean culture, while at the same time encouraging connections among the different communities in Montreal. In 2013, over 100 000 people joined in on the fun.

Montreal, Quebec

CARIBBEAN DAYS FESTIVAL
Vancouver

The Trinidad and Tobago Cultural Society (TTC) of British Columbia has hosted the Caribbean Days Festival every year since 1987. The waterfront festival features outdoor dance, an arts and clothing market, clothing market, an international food fair, a street parade, music, and a boat cruise. The parade is known for a lot of dancing, bright colours, and tropical music. The cruise features DJs and traditional Caribbean foods. The main stage of the festival hosts bands playing reggae, calypso, and international music. The TTC donates the money raised from the festival to a scholarship program for students entering post-secondary institutions. Over 60 000 people attend the two-day festival.

Vancouver, British Columbia

TORONTO CARIBBEAN CARNIVAL
Toronto

In 1967, 10 members of the Caribbean community in Toronto came up with the idea of a carnival to celebrate Caribbean culture. This colourful carnival consists of the Grand Parade, music, a king and queen, and the Junior Carnival. The Grand Parade is the main event of Toronto's Caribbean Carnival. People who join the parade are organized into bands. Each band has a theme. The theme can be history, politics, fantasy, and so on. People dress in costumes according to these themes. Their costumes feature bright colours, jewels, glitter, feathers, makeup, masks, and headdresses. The parade is 4.5 km long and can last between four and six hours. In 2013, about 10 000 people danced in the parade, and over one million people attended.

Men and women compete for the title of King and Queen. They are judged by their costumes and how well the costumes fit in with their theme. They are also judged by their dancing and performances.

CONNECT IT

Choose a celebration or tradition from your school, family, or community. Create a poster inviting the public to attend the celebration.

Toronto Caribbean Carnival

Index

Acknowledgements

The publisher gratefully acknowledges the following for permission to reprint copyrighted material in this book.

Anderson, Scott. "Africentric Schools," from *University of Toronto Magazine*, 11 September 2009. Copyright © 2013 University of Toronto. All rights reserved. Permission courtesy of Scott Anderson.

Goddard, John. "'We Don't Sell Tickets to Negroes,' they said," from *Toronto Star*, 16 February 2009. Reprinted by permission of Torstar Syndication Services.

Grimes, Nikki. "Beginnings," from *Planet Middle School* by Nikki Grimes. © 2011 by Nikki Grimes. Reprinted by permission of Bloomsbury Books for Young Readers.

Holland, Jackson. "Great-Great-Grandson Remembers Fugitive Slave Who Fled to Hamilton," from CBC News, 16 July 2012. Copyright © CBC 2014. All rights reserved.

Philip, Marlene Nourbese. Excerpt from *Harriet's Daughter*. Women's Press, 1988. Reprinted by permission of Three O'Clock Press.

"Toronto's 1st Africentric School," from CBC News, 4 September 2009. Copyright © CBC 2014. All rights reserved.

Photo Sources
Cover: hands–AJP/Shutterstock.com; **4–5:** [family–Yuri Arcurs; abstract–kstudija] Shutterstock.com; **6–9:** grunge background–ilolab/Shutterstock.com; **6:** Canada–Joe Iera/Shutterstock.com; **7:** painting–Library and Archives Canada, Acc. No. 1938-220-1; **8:** Amherstburg–Library and Archives Canada; Josiah Henson–ClassicStock.com/SuperStock; **9:** Amber Valley–© Glenbow Museum; Sir James Douglas–BC Archives; **10:** Africville–Ted Grant/Library and Archives Canada; **11:** Africville residents, people inside church–Nova Scotia Archives; **12:** rebuilt church–Hantsheroes; old church–Nova Scotia Archives;

13: paper–© IM/iStockphoto.com; **14–15:** Attic image–© vecstar/iStockphoto.com; **16–17:** [texture–Chyrko Olena, album–Lukiyanova Natalia/frenta] Shutterstock.com; **18–21:** [texture layer–vata; map–Nik Merkulov] Shutterstock.com; Holland family reunion photos–Glenn Lowson; **22–23:** kids–Jamie Wilson/Shutterstock.com; **24–29:** splashes–antart/Shutterstock.com; **24:** [girl–Monkey Business Images; Toronto–IVY PHOTOS] Shutterstock.com; **25:** [Tobago map–Rainer Lesniewski; palm trees–somchaij] Shutterstock.com; **26:** [chair–mike mols; chalkboard–bioraven] Shutterstock.com; **27:** [girl–Monkey Business Images; classroom–Pavel L Photo and Video] Shutterstock.com; **28:** [girl with backpack–Paul Hakimata Photography; fence–Sergej Razvodovskij] Shutterstock.com; **29:** [school bus–carroteater; girl–Monkey Business Images] Shutterstock.com; **30–31:** [ice–Dmitrydesign; tickets–Petr Vaclavek] Shutterstock.com; **31:** Donny Jubas and Harry Gairey–Toronto Star/GetStock.com; **32–33:** grey background–Catz/Shutterstock.com; **32:** Ware homestead–Velma Carter and LeVero (Lee) Carter.– Edmonton: Reidmore Books, c1989. – v, 82 p.; **34:** [baby–Flashon Studio; border–Mila Petkova; circular decorations–Silanti] Shutterstock.com **35:** family–Exactostock/SuperStock; **36–39:** spider body–© Antagain/iStockphoto.com; [spider legs– alslutsky; spider web–paprika] Shutterstock.com; **36:** [jungle–Sergey Uryadnikov; soil–ligio; landscape background–Jan Mastnik; rabbit–Stefan Petru Andronache; rabbit hole–SASIMOTO; spider–Aleksey Stemmer] Shutterstock.com; **37:** [lettuce–aida ricciardiello; pot–Aksenova Natalya; spider front legs up–fivespots; spoon–Ensuper; background–Piotr Krzeslak] Shutterstock.com; **38:** [straw background–Det-anan; hanging pot–SF photo; monkey–Art_man; forest–Lightspring; food–desk006; wood stick–Gyvafoto] Shutterstock.com; pig–© stray_cat/iStockphoto.com; **40–43:** Sheppard Public School–Tony Bock/Toronto Star/GetStock.com; **40:** pencil–rzstudio; girl–Horst Petzold] Shutterstock.com; **41:** [paper–Sarrote Sakwong; boys–Thomas M Perkins] Shutterstock.com; **42:** George Dei–Hans Deryk/GetStock.com; **44:** woman–arindambanerjee/Shutterstock.com; **45:** [people dancing–meunierd; Montreal–Alphonse Tran] Shutterstock.com; **46:** [Steel Band–EP photo; Vancouver–Josef Hanus] Shutterstock.com; **47:** Queen–Eduardo Zárat; Toronto–Lucy/Shutterstock.com.